Football

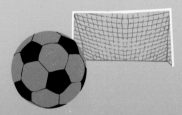

First published in 2011
by Wayland

Copyright © Wayland 2011

Wayland
338 Euston Road
London NW1 3BH

Wayland Australia
Level 17/207 Kent Street
Sydney, NSW 2000

Series Editor: Louise John
Editor: Katie Woolley
Design: D.R.ink
Consultant: Shirley Bickler
Photographer: Andy Crawford

A CIP catalogue record for this book is available
from the British Library.

ISBN 9780750264976

Printed in China

Wayland is a division of Hachette Children's Books,
an Hachette UK Company

www.hachette.co.uk

The Publisher and author would like to thank all the models who took part in this book.

Contents

My football club

My name is Freddie and today I am going to football club.

Getting ready

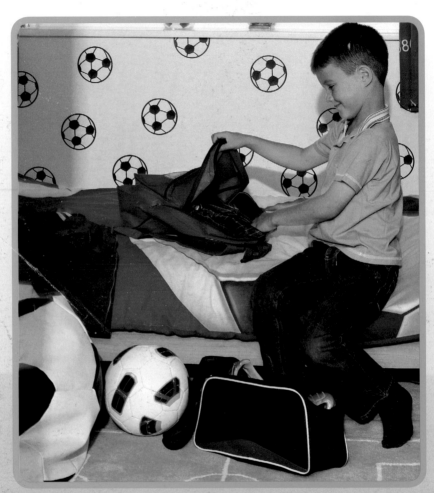

I pack my boots and a tracksuit for later.

When I am in my football kit and ready to go, my sister gives me a drink and a snack.

The ground

Dad has brought me to football today.

My club plays at the local ground. I go every Saturday morning for an hour.

Top Tips

It is important to drink water regularly when doing exercise.

The coach

My coach Richard says hello to Dad. He asks Dad if he is going to stay and watch us play today.

"Yes!" says Dad. He tells me to have fun.

Meeting my friends

I go to join my friends Matt and Alex.
I see them at football club every week.

We sit on the grass and wait for everyone to arrive. Today we talk about a football match we saw last week.

Dribbling

We all sit down and listen to Richard. He tells us that we are going to practise our dribbling skills today.

Richard is a really good footballer. He trains in schools and runs three clubs.

The warm-up

We always start with a warm-up. We have to jog around and stay on our toes.

Then we have to jog on the spot and lift our knees.

Top Tips

Always warm up and cool down before and after matches.

17

Stretches

Next we do our stretches. We stretch our leg and arm muscles.

Richard says stretching is
really important. It helps to
stop us getting hurt when we
are playing.

Skills practice

After warm-up we do our skills practice. Today we are using the cones. We have to dribble the ball around them.

Sometimes Richard puts the cones closer together. This makes it harder!

Top Tips

Try to keep your head up when you dribble. Then you can see what is going on around you.

British Bulldog

We usually play a running game next.
We are playing "British Bulldog" today.
It is one of my favourites. Alex is bulldog
and we all have to try to catch him.

Now it is my turn to be bulldog and the others have to try to catch me.

The match

We always end with a mini match.
Richard splits us up into two teams.
He gives us green or orange vests to wear.

He blows his whistle
and we kick off.

25

Goal!

I am on the orange team. It's a good match, but there are no goals yet.

26

The match is almost over when
I score the winning goal! I can
hear Dad cheering.

Player of the day

It feels great when Richard
makes me player of the day.

28

I am really pleased that Dad was watching today. He shows me a photograph he took when I scored.

Time to go home

It is time to go home. I tell Matt and Alex I will see them next week. They say, "Well done for scoring that goal!"

I always look forward to football club.
It is the best bit of the week!

START READING is a series of highly enjoyable books for beginner readers. **The books have been carefully graded to match the Book Bands widely used in schools.** This enables readers to be sure they choose books that match their own reading ability.

Look out for the Band colour on the book in our Start Reading logo.

The Bands are:

Pink Band 1A & 1B

Red Band 2

Yellow Band 3

Blue Band 4

Green Band 5

Orange Band 6

Turquoise Band 7

Purple Band 8

Gold Band 9

START READING books can be read independently or shared with an adult. They promote the enjoyment of reading through satisfying stories, plays and non-fiction narratives, which are supported by fun illustrations and photographs.

Jillian Powell has written many fiction and non-fiction books for children. She began writing stories when she was just four years old and she hasn't stopped since! She lives in a house beside a village church and still sits down to write every day.

Seasons of the year

Jilly Attwood

Heinemann
LIBRARY

Little Nippers

www.heinemann.co.uk/library
Visit our website to find out more information about **Heinemann Library** books.

To order:
☎ Phone 44 (0) 1865 888066
🖹 Send a fax to 44 (0) 1865 314091
🖳 Visit the Heinemann Bookshop at www.heinemann.co.uk/library to browse our catalogue and order online.

First published in Great Britain by Heinemann Library, Halley Court, Jordan Hill, Oxford OX2 8EJ, part of Harcourt Education.
Heinemann is a registered trademark of Harcourt Education Ltd.

Editorial: Kathy Peltan and Kate Bellamy
Design: Jo Hinton-Malivoire and Bigtop, Bicester, UK
Picture Research: Ruth Blair
Production: Séverine Ribierre

Originated by Dot Gradations Ltd
Printed and bound in China by South China Printing Company

ISBN 0 431 07940 4 (hardback)
09 08 07 06 05
10 9 8 7 6 5 4 3 2 1

ISBN 0 431 07945 5 (paperback)
09 08 07 06 05
10 9 8 7 6 5 4 3 2 1

British Library Cataloguing in Publication Data
Attwood, Jilly
508.2
Talking about time: Seasons of the year
A full catalogue record for this book is available from the British Library.

Acknowledgements
The publishers would like to thank the following for permission to reproduce photographs: Corbis pp. **4**, **9**, **11**, **13**, **19**, **21**, **23**; Digital Vision p. **12** (Rob Van Petten); Getty Images/Photodisc pp. **5a**, **5b**, **6**, **10**, **14**, **18**; Getty Images p. **22**; Getty Images/Digital Vision p. **16-17**; Harcourt Education p. **7**, **15**; Harcourt Education pp. **4a** (Peter Evans), **8** (Trevor Clifford).

Cover photograph of children playing in autumn leaves, reproduced with permission of Getty Images (Digital Vision).

Our thanks to Annie Davy for her assistance in the preparation of this book.

Every effort has been made to contact copyright holders of any material reproduced in this book. Any omissions will be rectified in subsequent printings if notice is given to the publishers.

...s book comes from

Contents

Seasons of the year

There are **four** seasons of the year.

2 Summer

1 Spring

4

3 Autumn

4 Winter

Do you know what they are called?

It's spring!

In spring there is sunshine and showers.

If there is sun and rain at the same time you might get a rainbow!

6

What do you wear when it is raining?

What happens in spring?

Many plants start to **grOW** in spring.

8

Many animals have babies in spring.

Baaa!

9

It's summer!

Summer is the **hottest** time of the year.

When the air gets too **hot** there can be **big** thunderstorms.

Crash!
Bang!

Eating out

It's fun to eat outside when it is warm.

In the summer there is lots of fruit to eat!

Don't eat them all!

It can be **cold** and frosty in the morning.

What do you wear when it is cool?

Autumn fun

What do you like to do in autumn?

Do you like to play in the leaves?

17

It's winter!

Winter is the coldest time of the year.

Most plants don't grow in winter.

It's a snow day!

In some places it snows in winter!

It's fun playing
in the snow.

21

Four seasons

Do you know what order the seasons happen in?

Index

Notes for adults

The *Talking about time* series introduces young children to the concept of time. By relating their own experiences to specific moments in time, the children can start to explore the pattern of regular events that occur in a day, week or year. The following Early Learning Goals are relevant to this series:

Knowledge and understanding of the world
Early learning goals for a sense of time
• find out about past and present events in their own lives, and in those of their families and other people they know
Early learning goals for exploration and investigation
• look closely at similarities, differences, patterns and change
Early learning goals for cultures and beliefs
• describe significant events for family or friends

This book describes what happens in the natural world during each of the four seasons of the year. The text is supported by photographs showing children doing activities typical to each season. As the seasons are presented chronologically, the book encourages children to observe the cyclical nature of the world around them and to build up a sense of how long a season is. It also encourages discussion about how weather determines the clothes children wear and the activities they do throughout the year.

Follow-up activities
• Make regular observations about what happens in nature in every season. Keep a 'seasons' book to record changes.
• Talking about what clothes it would be appropriate to wear in different weather, and why.
• Grow plants in spring, and talk about why plants start to grow in spring, and how long it takes for the seed to become a plant.

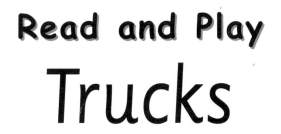

Read and Play
Trucks

by Jim Pipe

Aladdin/Watts
London • Sydney

truck

2

This is a **truck**.

It carries a heavy load.

3

driver

4

A truck has a **driver**.

The **driver** sits in the cab.

5

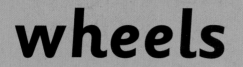
wheels

6

A truck has **wheels**.

Wheels help a truck move.

7

engine

8

A truck has an **engine**.

The **engine** makes it strong.

9

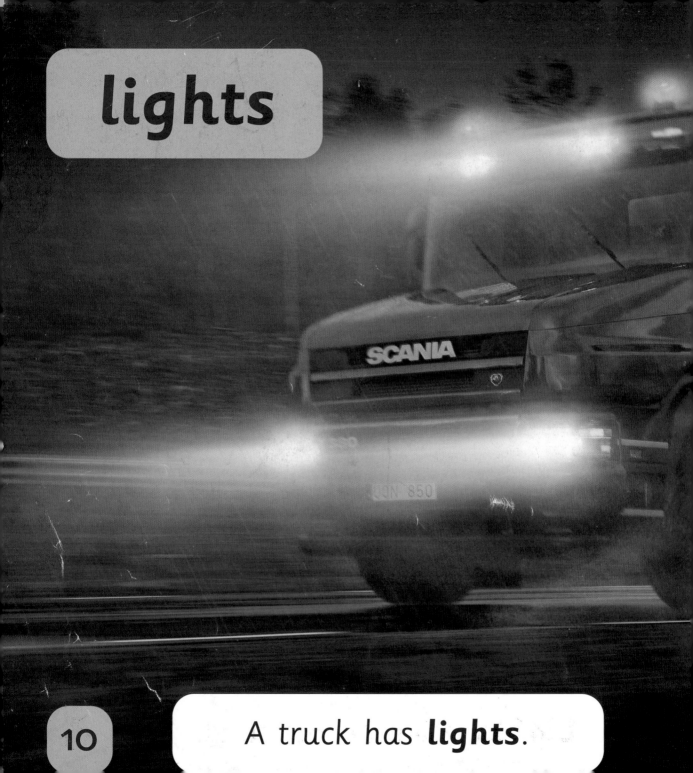

lights

10

A truck has **lights**.

Lights shine on the road.

11

small

This is a **small** truck.

big

This is a very **big** truck.

13

tip

14

This is a **tipper** truck.

It **tips** its load.

15

fire

A **fire** engine puts out **fires**.

This truck clears **snow**.

snow

17

slow

18 This giant truck is very **slow**.

fast

This truck is very **fast**.

19

What am I?

lights

driver

wheel

cab

20 Match the words and pictures.

How many?

Can you count the trucks?

21

What do I do?

22 What jobs do these trucks do?

Index

Can you find these truck pictures in the book?

For Parents and Teachers

Questions you could ask:

p. 2 What colour is the truck? e.g. red/silver. Point out shiny parts, black tyres, windows etc and discuss what materials they are made from.

p. 6 How many wheels can you see? Compare with the number of wheels on other trucks. Remember there are wheels on both sides of truck!

p. 9 What is this truck carrying? e.g. logs. Compare with other loads, e.g. digger, goods, soil etc.

p. 10 When does a driver turn on the lights? e.g. at night. You could also ask what colour the lights are at the back of a truck, e.g. red/yellow.

p. 13 How big is this truck? Point out the man at the front and ask the reader to guess the height, e.g. the truck is as tall as three people.

p. 15 What sound does a truck's horn make? Point out the two horns on top of the cab.

p. 17 Where does the water come from? The fire engine carries the water to the fire. Point out the long hose connected to the fire engine.

p. 18 What is the giant truck carrying? e.g. space shuttle/rocket. The truck moves very slowly as the rocket is very heavy. For scale, note the tiny figure walking alongside the transporter.

Activities you could do:

• Ask the reader to act out driving in a truck, e.g. starting the engine, turning steering wheel, blowing horn, braking, making suitable noises!

• When they are out and about, e.g. on a car journey, ask the reader to spot different kinds of trucks and the jobs that they do.

• Look at how wheels work indoors and outdoors, e.g. on bikes, trolleys, buggies and toy cars.

• Encourage the reader to sing action rhymes such as "The Wheels on the Bus".

• Use recycled materials to create models of trucks, e.g. fire engine, tipper truck. Include circular items such as foil dishes and plastic lids for wheels.

Paperback Edition 2009
© Aladdin Books Ltd 2006

Designed and produced by
Aladdin Books Ltd
PO Box 53987
London SW15 2SF

First published in 2006
by Franklin Watts
338 Euston Road
London NW1 3BH

Franklin Watts Australia
Level 17/207 Kent Street
Sydney NSW 2000

Franklin Watts is a division of Hachette Children's Books, an Hachette Livre UK company.
www.hachettelivre.co.uk

ISBN 978 0 7496 8978 0

A catalogue record for this book is available from the British Library.

Dewey Classification: 629.224

Printed in Malaysia

Series consultant
Zoe Stillwell is an experienced Early Years teacher currently teaching at Pewley Down Infant School, Guildford.

Photocredits:
l-left, r-right, b-bottom, t-top, c-centre, m-middle
1, 4, 6-7, 8, 10-11, 16, 17, 20tr & tl, 21, 22tr — Scania. 2-3, 14-15 — photos courtesy of Mack Trucks, Inc. 5, 12, 13, 20br & bl, 22b — istockfoto.com. 9 — Corbis. 18 — NASA. 19 — US Navy. 22tr — Photodisc.